Reptile Keeper's Guides

BEARDED DRAGONS

R. D. Bartlett
Patricia P. Bartlett

BARRON'S

Acknowledgments

For shared knowledge and photographic opportunities, we extend our heartfelt appreciation to Karin Burns and Billy Griswold (Next Generation Reptiles), hobbyists Liz Craig and Matthew Steen, Bert and Hester Langerwerf (Agama International), Bill and Kathy Love (Blue Chameleon Ventures), Buzz Ross, Peter and Phyllis Weis (Weis Reptiles), and Rob MacInnes (Glades Herp).

Although our chart on medication was provided by Richard Funk, DVM, we also owe our sincerest thanks to Fredric Frye, DVM, for his comments on medications and other aspects of this manuscript.

All inquiries should be addressed to:
Barron's Educational Series, Inc.
250 Wireless Boulevard
Hauppauge, NY 11788
http://www.barronseduc.com

International Standard Book No. 0-7641-1125-6
Library of Congress Catalog Card No. 99-26239

Library of Congress Cataloging-in-Publication Data

Bartlett, Richard D., 1938–
    Bearded dragons / R.D. and Patricia Bartlett.
        p. cm. — (Reptile basics)
    ISBN 0-7641-1125-6
    1. Bearded dragons (Reptiles) as pets. I. Bartlett, Patricia Pope, 1949–.
II. Title. III. Series: Bartlett, Richard D., 1938–. Reptile Keeper's Guides.
SF459.L5B364 1999
639.3'95—dc21   99-26239
                                                                          CIP

Printed in Hong Kong
98

Contents

Preface

This book is designed to help you with the husbandry of one of today's most popular pet lizards, the bearded dragon, and, in particular, the inland bearded dragon. It includes husbandry and dietary information for these Australian omnivores. Fortunately, bearded dragons are also one of the easier lizards to provide for and are relatively confiding and responsive to their keepers. They have interesting territorial displays, attain a moderate size, and can be kept in relatively small quarters. If their basic needs are met, they can be easily captive bred for several seasons and will live for 7 to 10+ years. Because virtually all dragons now available in the American pet trade are bred in captivity, you don't need to worry about any impact on wild populations.

We hope that you will enjoy your bearded dragon, and that the information we have provided will make it just a little easier to understand your pet lizard.

Dick and Patti Bartlett
Gainesville, Florida, U.S.A.

Introduction

Until a few years ago, were you to mention your pet bearded dragon to an American hobbyist, most would have looked askance. However, today, this Australian lizard not only is rather well known but is also considered one of the best lizards in the American pet trade. It tames down easily, usually remains tame, and is responsive to its owner. It consumes a wide variety of easily obtainable foods. It is large enough to handle easily. It breeds readily in captivity and has large numbers of young.

The dominant bearded dragon of the American pet trade is the inland bearded dragon, *Pogona vitticeps*. It is actually just one of eight species. The whats, whys, and wherefores of this popularity are what we will discuss in these pages.

This inland dragon is fully relaxed.

What Is the Bearded Dragon?

The bearded dragons (some species of which have no beards) are heavy-bodied and quietly attractive Australian lizards. They have a quiet and confiding nature and seem unafraid of and very responsive to their keepers.

All are in the genus *Pogona* (formerly *Amphibolurus*) in the family Agamidae. At least four of the eight species of these lizards are captive bred in some numbers. The most popular member of the genus is the inland bearded dragon, *P. vitticeps*, a large species, now captive bred by the thousands of specimens annually. This is the species about which most is known.

As a group, bearded dragons are arid-dwelling, heliothermic (sun-basking), heat-tolerant lizards. Body temperatures of basking lizards may exceed 100° F. When cold, dragons become reclusive and inactive. Although often seen on the ground, bearded dragons easily ascend fence posts, dead trees, anthills, and other such low-elevation positions to bask and display. The most dominant males usually assume the most prominent positions. A curious arm-waving, called circumduction, is exhibited by both young and adults and apparently serves as an appeasement gesture. The gesture is used particularly often by subadult and adult female lizards.

The beard is flared when male inland bearded dragons display.

The beards are used by both sexes as a part of the courtship and territorial displays, although the beards of the males are larger and usually much darker. Beards are darkest during periods of reproductive activity. The beards are quickly displayed or distended by a forward motion of the hyoid structure in the throat, and both sexes bob their heads as part of this display. Males bob more quickly than females. All bearded dragons are oviparous. The smaller species are primarily insectivorous, but the larger forms are quite omnivorous, feeding in the wild on vegetation such as dandelions and other flowers, beetles, and a variety of seeds.

Meet the Eight Bearded Dragons

The inland bearded dragon, *P. vitticeps*, is a spectacular lizard that has gone from comparative obscurity to ready pet shop availability in only a decade. In its native habitat, it is common over much of arid and semi-arid southeastern Australia. At an adult length of 18–22 in., it is marginally shorter than some other *Pogona*

species, but it is more robust. In the wild, it is found amid eucalypti and acacias, in brushlands, on sandy and rocky plains, and amid short grasses. It may be seen basking and displaying from elevated rocks, tree trunks, and fence posts. Its ground color varies from tan to gray to brick red and usually blends well with the soils on which it is found. Broad, lighter paravertebral lines and some degree of dorsal blotching are usually present, although older males may be nearly unicolored. It is quite capable of moving rapidly but may depend on its cryptic appearance to evade detection.

Wayne Van Devender recently related to us his experiences in sighting a large inland dragon in New South Wales. The lizard darted away as it was approached and seemed to disappear. After a considerable search, the lizard was resighted. It was nearly invisible where it lay, hunched and with closed eyes, amidst a field of cow "patties."

The inland bearded's evolution as a desert lizard is revealed in its behavior when kept in a terrarium with proper heating and lighting choices. When it basks, its body temperature may exceed 100° F. It enjoys basking atop elevated limbs and rocks and will

This inland dragon is warm, still basking, and moderately alert.

utilize a brightly lit basking area having a surface temperature of 110–115° F. As with the other species of bearded dragons, the most dominant male usually assumes the most prominent position.

Young sexually mature inland dragon females can be amazingly prolific. In captivity, large, well-fed females may produce over 150 eggs a year (occasionally with more than 35 in a clutch).

Pogona barbata, the coastal bearded dragon, is not as popular or as readily available as the inland bearded, but captive-born stock is available. This is marginally the largest species. It may reach a length of 22 in., with just over half the length being tail. This is generally the species darkest in coloration, with some being almost charcoal in ground color. Other specimens may have a ground color of buff or sand red. Enlarged conical spines adorn the beard of this species, making the breeding display especially impressive. The mouth is opened as part of the display, and the bright lemon to mustard lining is an impressive sight. Although eastern bearded dragons are occasionally available to hobbyists, they are consid-

ered a little more difficult to keep and breed than the inland bearded dragon.

Pogona barbata is found in wooded parts of eastern Australia. Near Sydney, during cooler weather, the eastern bearded has been found to overwinter by secreting itself into burrows beneath rocks and hibernating. Because it is adapted to habitats along Australia's relatively humid east coast, the eastern bearded dragon might be the best choice for hobbyists located in humid areas. It is somewhat more arboreal than the other dragons, readily ascending and basking atop higher brush piles, leaning trees, fence posts, and similar vantage points. Its diet is the same as the inland bearded dragon.

Two small "beardless" bearded dragons complete the list of bearded dragon species currently available in American and European herpeticulture. The first, the (beardless) dwarf bearded dragon, *Pogona minor*, is less popular in America than in Europe. Its adult size is just over a foot in length. It occurs widely in the arid lands of Western Australia, western South Australia, and southwestern Northern Territory. The second beardless species is the lesser bearded dragon, *Pogona henrylawsoni*. It is

Coastal bearded dragons are dark in color and have a characteristic yellow mouth lining.

second only to the inland bearded dragon in popularity, but this is not meant to indicate that it is common in collections. In size, the lesser bearded dragon may reach 14 in. in length. (You may see this lizard listed under two erroneous names, *P. rankeni* and *P. brevis.* The common name of Lawson's dragon is also often applied.)

The lesser bearded dragon comes from central Queensland, Australia. It has been hybridized with the inland bearded dragon, and the young are marketed as vittikens dragons, and are occasionally provided the erroneous and invalid name of *Pogona vittikens* on dealers' price lists.

The four remaining described species of bearded dragons are all quietly colored in sandy hues, and most have prominent dorsal banding and/or blotching. The patterns are often best developed on juveniles of both sexes and adult females.

The western bearded dragon is scientifically known as *Pogona minima,* and it is captive bred in the United States and Europe in small numbers. It is still considered a race of the dwarf bearded dragon, *P. minor,* by some authorities. The western bearded is a 13-in. long dragon, found in a very restricted area of the western part of Western Australia. It has a well-defined row of lateral spines and enlarged head spines of disparate sizes.

The small-scaled dragon, *Pogona microlepidota,* is one of the less spiny of this genus of very spiny lizards. It is one of the larger species, attaining an overall length of about 18 in., and is found in a small area of coastal northern Western Australia. It lacks prominent nuchal spines and enlarged spines in the center of the throat. As far as we know, no specimens of the small-scaled dragon or of the follow-

The parent species of this "vittikins" dragon are the inland and the lesser bearded dragon. The hybrid can attain a 15-in. length.

The lesser bearded dragon, *P. henrylawsoni,* a medium-sized species, has undergone a great deal of taxonomic confusion.

ing two species have been reported in the United States.

Mitchell's dragon, *Pogona mitchelli,* is a 14-in. long species that inhabits the more arid northern regions of Western Australia and adjacent Northern Territory. It was long considered a race of *P. minor,* the dwarf bearded dragon. Mitchell's dragon tends to have a large, orangish head and two clusters of nuchal spines.

The fourth species, *Pogona nullarbor,* is referred to as the Nullarbor Plain bearded dragon. It occurs in the arid Nullabor Plains region in southeastern Western Australia and adjacent South Australia. It is adult at about 13 in. in total length and lacks clusters of nuchal spines. Its head is not as noticeably broadened as some

other species, and it lacks noticeably enlarged gular (chin) spines.

Longevity

Although the life spans of the various dragons are virtually unreported on in the wild, those of captives are somewhat better known. Compared to some lizards, the bearded dragons do not seem particularly long-lived. Many accounts exist, for both the small and large dragon species, of longevity only in the 5- to 6-year range.

An eastern bearded dragon, wild-collected as an adult, lived as a captive for 9 years and 11 months. And with a known maximum age of 10 years and 1 month, the inland bearded dragon is marginally the longest lived.

This red flame dragon is basking in the shelter of a log.

The Bearded Dragon as a Pet

Choosing a Healthy Bearded Dragon

When you select your bearded dragon, choose a specimen that is lively and alert. If at all possible, choose one that seems unafraid of being handled. Although there isn't much difference in personality between the males and females, the males are by nature more outgoing than the females.

Handling Your Dragon
Providing it is done gently, inland bearded dragons quickly become tolerant of handling. Adults are more tolerant than juveniles. Despite their being

Inland bearded dragons are among the most easily handled of lizards. They will usually sit quietly on a hand or arm.

much easier to handle than many other lizards, it is still a good idea to restrain bearded dragons when you are holding them outdoors. Even when lying quietly on your shoulder or arm, if startled, a dragon will drop to the ground and scamper rapidly away. If allowed to fall for more than a short distance, injury can occur. When lifting a dragon, support it adequately, encircling its body with your hand and allowing it to hold your fingers with its claws.

Sexing Your Dragon
It is virtually impossible to sex a baby bearded dragon accurately. If you buy a baby, and if the sex is important to you, ask your supplier if you can exchange the animal if it turns out not to the be sex you wanted. If you're buying an adult bearded, the sexing process is somewhat easier.

Male adult dragons have a wider tail base. When the cloacal opening is exposed by pulling back the skin around the vent, the cloacal opening for the males is wider than for the females. Males have a broader, more strongly triangular head than the females. When gravid, the basic body shape of the female is heavier than that of the male. Displaying males have a darker beard (especially during

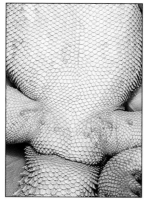

Bearded dragons are not always easy to sex. Females (left) have insignificant femoral and preanal pores, whereas those of the male are irregular but larger.

the breeding season). The femoral and preanal pores of the males—the pores on the underside of each femor and anterior to the vent—are darker and larger than the femoral pores of the females. Males have more aggressive behavior during the breeding season, which means that they more readily flare out their beards and open their mouths when you open the cage. (This display is meant to intimidate other beardeds and does not count as aggression toward their keeper, although some dragons will bite.) Females often use circumduction rather than beard displays.

Hemipenes of both juveniles and adult males can be "popped," or rolled out using pressure from your thumb, but this can be potentially injurious to the lizards. We strongly urge that this be done only by those experienced in the technique.

Obtaining Your Bearded Dragon

Depending on their color, bearded dragons can vary in purchase price from relatively inexpensive to quite expensive. Those offered most frequently by pet stores are usually a generic tan to brown in color, but may exhibit many earthen hues in between. Because the eagerly sought brilliantly colored morphs—red-headed, gold-headed, sandfire, etc.—are considerably more expensive than the more normally colored specimens, you may need to special-order through your local pet store or go to a specialty dealer/breeder. The special color morphs are often well represented at reptile expos that feature captive-bred specimens.

Although these are usually easily kept reptiles, we urge you to hone your husbandry skills on one or two of the less expensive bearded dragons before you acquire the more costly colored morphs of bearded dragons.

Pet Stores
If given even modest care, bearded dragons will easily withstand the rigors of pet store life, and there certainly could hardly be anything more convenient than the acquisition of your dragon from a neighborhood source. In fact, in the last few years, bearded dragons have become a staple

in the larger pet stores. Bearded dragons, like iguanas, are almost always available. We advocate shopping at pet stores because of the convenience and because it gives you the opportunity to discuss your potential purchase, one-on-one, with a knowledgable store employee. Such things as routine care are easily covered.

But there are some things that your pet store cannot be expected to know. Among others are the actual origins, or genetics, of a given specimen. Remember that your local pet shop is often two or even three or four times removed from the initial dealing that placed the specimen in the pet trade. The employee can only repeat what he or she has been told by the supplier.

Reptile and Amphibian Expos

Herp expos came into being about a decade ago. They are now held in many larger cities across the United States and are becoming popular in Europe. It seems that there is at least one occurring at some point in the United States on any given weekend. An expo is merely the commercial gathering of dealers, breeders, and hobbyists, all under one roof. The expo may vary in size from the 450+ tables of the National Reptile Breeders' Expo in Orlando, Florida, every August to others that are much smaller but almost as comprehensive. Bearded dragons, in all existing colors, are available at nearly every expo.

Breeders

Breeders may vary in size from spare-room hobbyists who produce only a few clutches of bearded dragons annually to commercial breeders who produce literally thousands of hatchlings. With each passing year, more and more breeders present the fruits of their labors at herp expos, but there are many who prefer to sell in other ways. Refer to the classified or pictorial ads sections in specialty reptile and amphibian magazines (see the Special Interest Groups section, page 42) or even the classified ads in your local paper. Breeders, especially one living near you, can offer healthy, well-acclimated baby dragons, as well as an occasional large specimen and accurate husbandry information. Most keep records of genetics, lineage, fecundity,

In preparation for sleeping, dragons may partially or completely bury themselves in the sand. (photo by Billy Griswold)

health, and quirks of the individual lizards with which they work.

There are some breeders, like Bert and Hester Langerwerf (Agama International, Montevallo, AL) who concentrate on breeding large numbers of normal colored dragons for the pet trade. Others like Bob Mailloux (Sandfire Dragon Ranch, Bonsall, CA) and Pete and Phyllis Weis (Weis Reptiles, Tallahassee, FL) produce normal colored pet trade dragons and also selectively breed for enhanced colors and patterns.

Specialty Dealers

The continuing popularity of reptiles has allowed the development of specialty dealers. Besides often breeding fair numbers of the reptiles they offer, specialty dealers deal directly with other breeders (across the world) and may even be direct importers. Imported specimens are usually acclimated to some extent, have been fed, and often are subjected to a veterinary checkup. Many such dealers both buy and sell reptiles and amphibians at herp expos.

Mail-Order Purchase and Shipping

If you are a little off the beaten path, and if your local pet store cannot supply you with the bearded dragon you want, mail order may be the answer.

How does one go about ordering a bearded dragon by mail? How does one even learn that a particular morph or species of bearded dragon is available? Let's explore mail-order purchases and shipping. There are several ways to learn of the availability of the particular morph of bearded dragon in which you are interested.

When seen next to each other, the color differences of this orange tiger (above) and this red flame inland dragon (below) are obvious.

- World Wide Web: By instructing your search engine to seek "bearded dragons," you should learn of several hundred breeders and suppliers, many of whom have excellent photos on their web sites.

- Classified ads: Dealers and hobbyists list their available livestock in the classified ads of the *Reptile and Amphibian Hobbyist Magazine* and other pet magazines.
- Word of mouth: Ask friends and fellow enthusiasts for recommendations about the reptile dealers they know. Try to check what you hear by asking at nature centers, museums, and zoos or among hobbyist groups. Herpetoculture is a close-knit hobby. You'll be surprised by how many of us know each other.

What next? After learning that your potential supplier has a satisfactory reputation, request a price list (often available automatically on the web). Decide what, if anything, you are going to purchase, and contact your breeder/supplier to finalize details.

What is involved with shipping? The shipping of reptiles is not at all the insurmountable barrier that many hobbyists initially think it to be. But it can be expensive. The chances are excellent that the supplier you have chosen to use is quite familiar with shipping and will be delighted to assist you in any way possible.

Among the things on which you and your shipper will have to agree are the method of payment and the method and date of shipping.

Payment

The price you are quoted for your lizards is just that—only for the animals themselves. Shipping charges will be extra. The method of payment should be agreed upon and fully understood by both you, the purchaser, and the shipper at the time of ordering. Unless the shipper knows you well, he or she will almost always insist that the specimen be paid for in full (including boxing charges, a fee for the actual shipping container) prior to shipment. This may be done with a money order, cashier's check, or a credit card. Most shippers will accept personal checks but will not ship until the check has cleared their bank (usually a week or so after deposit).

An alternate method of payment is C.O.D.; however, this can be expensive and inconvenient. Most airlines will accept cash only (not a check, not a credit card) for the C.O.D. amount, and there is a hefty C.O.D. surcharge fee (upward of $15) in addition to all other charges.

Methods of Shipping

There are options available for shipping lizards that are not available for shipping snakes or turtles. Some are:

- Express mail: If you choose to use this door-to-door service, your shipper will require payment in advance. The cost is $15 to $25, and live-delivery may not be guaranteed.
- Air freight: Depending on the airline used, either two or three levels of service are available for this airport-to-airport service. Regular, space-available freight, where the shipping charges are paid when you pick up the animal (this is also called charges collect), will cost about $35. Air Express, which provides guaranteed flights and charges collect, will cost about $70. Special Handling, with guaranteed flights and charges prepaid will cost about $55.
- Other options: Occasionally shipping companies such as Airborne or FedEx will accept lizards (this is the local manager's prerogative at the

shipping origination site). Charges are prepaid and vary between $15 and $40 for this door-to-door service.

Someone must be at your home to sign for the package on any of the door-to-door services.

Shipping

Your supplier will need your full name, address, and current day and night telephone numbers. Inform your shipper of the airport you wish to use, or agree on a door-to-door delivery company. If your area of the country is serviced by more than one airport (such as the areas around Washington, DC, New York City, or San Francisco), be very specific about which airport you wish to use.

Agree on a date and get an air bill number. Avoid weekend arrivals when the cargo offices at most small airports are closed. Some shippers go to the airport only on one or two specific days each week. Work out a shipping date in advance. Allow enough time for your shipment to get to you before panicking. Most shipments take about 24 hours to get from the airport of origin to the airport of destination. It may take less time if you are lucky enough to be served by direct flights, it may take more time if you're in an area with limited flights and the shipment has to be transferred several times. Keep your shipment "on line" whenever possible. With live animals, you pay for each airline involved in the transportation. Ship only during "good" weather. Your dragons run added risks of shipping delays or other problems when the weather is very hot or cold or during the peak holiday travel/shipping/mailing times.

Choose a level of shipping. You will pay premium rates for either Air Express or Special Handling services, but they may be required by the airline if shipping conditions are adverse. Compare airlines. Some carriers charge up to twice as much as others for the same level of service.

After a reasonable time, call the airline that your shipment is traveling on and ask them for the status of the shipment. The airline will need the air bill number you were given to trace the shipment in their computer.

Pick up your shipment up as quickly after its arrival as possible. This is especially important in bad weather. Learn the hours of your cargo office and whether the shipment can be picked up at the ticket counter if it arrives after the cargo office has closed.

You will have to pay for your shipment (including all C.O.D. charges and fees) before you can inspect it. Once you are given your shipment, open it before leaving the cargo facility. Unless otherwise specified, reliable shippers guarantee live-delivery. However, to substantiate the existence of a problem, both shippers and airlines will require a "discrepancy" or "damage" report made out, signed, and dated by airline personnel. In the very rare case when a problem has occurred, insist on the filing of a claim form, and contact your shipper immediately for instructions.

After the first time, you will no longer find the shipping of specimens intimidating. Understanding the system will open new doors of acquisition.

The Colors of the Inland Bearded Dragon

In appearance, hatchlings of all the color phases mentioned here are very similar. It is not until they are more than one-third grown that coloration begins to brighten. Adult males tend to be brighter in general coloration and/or less well patterned than females. Additionally, a given dragon may vary significantly in color according to temperature and mood. Dragons are usually at their most brilliant when at optimal body temperature, dominant, and displaying, but they may also be quite brightly colored when sleeping soundly after darkness. Some females may have black(ish) beards, but there is usually white scale-tipping, whereas the beards of the males are dark overall. Dragons of both sexes darken beard colors when displaying and at other times of peak alertness.

Normal
This morph has a variable ground color of tan, brownish, grayish, or, more rarely, olive green. The face is banded, and the dorsolateral markings are lighter.

Red Flame
This well-patterned morph is still being enhanced by its developer, Peter Weis. Facial markings are prominent. The ground color is orangish tan to buff, and the dorsolateral blotches are a more brilliant orange to orange red. The area at the angle of the jaws is often brilliant orange.

Dragons readily change color, darkening when cold and brightening as they warm.

Inland bearded dragons often blend well with the sandy backgrounds of their cages.

Orange Tiger

This dragon has a yellow to orange body and broad, very dark, strongly contrasting lateral bands.

Sandfire

Developed at Sandfire Dragon Ranch by Bob Mailloux, most females are brilliantly colored but retain a prominent pattern. Pattern, including facial stripes, fades to virtual obscurity on aging males. The color may be goldish orange, orange, or orange red. Against this brilliance, the black beard of a breeding male is particularly evident.

Golden Headed

This name is self-descriptive. The body color is usually browner than the head color. This morph often has a white iris.

Red Headed

Like the golden-headed dragon, the name of this color phase is self-descriptive. The dragon's body is pale, whereas the head is brilliant red.

German Giant

This is a large, heavy-bodied, grayish dragon, which is probably a hybrid between the eastern and the inland dragons. It seems especially hardy and is, according to Peter Weis, remarkably resistant to the coccidial problems that may occasionally plague dragons.

Pastel

This phase, also a creation of Sandfire Dragon Ranch, has an orange-red head and a grayish blue or grayish pink (almost opalescent) body, legs, feet, and tail.

Sandfire dragons have reduced pattern and a bright ground color.

Peter Weis holds a German giant bearded dragon, a morph that is dull in color but prolific. It is, apparently, a hybrid between the inland and the coastal dragons.

Caging for Your Dragons

Bearded dragons are arid-land to semi-arid-land lizards. Most are primarily terrestrial, but they will climb any elevated vantage point. From these king-of-the-mountain positions, males and females thermoregulate and indulge in territorial and other displays. Although dragons are often thought of as indoor pets, where climatic conditions are arid and warm enough, they will thrive in outside cages. You may want to consider using outdoor caging during the summer months and switching to indoor caging during the cooler months.

Whether indoors or out, the size of the dragon cage should vary according to the sizes and number of the dragons kept therein. For a trio of adult inland bearded dragons, one male and two females, we suggest a cage with a floor that measures at least 1.5 ft. by 4 ft. This floor is about the same size as that of a 50-gallon aquarium. A larger terrarium would be even better. From one to a trio of dwarf bearded dragons could be successfully housed in a 30-gallon tank (with a 1.5 ft. by 3 ft. floor), but they would utilize a far larger tank were it to be provided. A larger colony of dragons would require additional floor space.

It might seem that baby or immature dragons could be kept in a smaller tank than the adults, but because baby dragons tend to be more aggressive toward their cage mates than the adults are, allowing proportionately more cage space would be even better for the juveniles.

When kept colonially, adult dragons become territorial and estab-

A dragon cage need not be extravagant but must provide the basics.

Dragons alertly watch the movement of their keepers.

lish a hiearchy. Once males have become sexually mature, it is usually not possible to keep more than one to a cage. Females will also work out a pattern of dominance, and the most dominant specimen may become persistently aggressive.

Substrates

Despite the conventional wisdom that sand is an unsatisfactory substrate for bearded dragons, we have used smooth (not sharp silica) sand as a substrate for desert lizards for years without mishap. We recommend a sand substrate for any naturalistic terrarium. Other substrates might be newspaper or Kraft paper (neither provides good traction), Astroturf, or indoor/outdoor carpeting. No matter the substrate, it must be kept scrupulously clean. Although some hobbyists have voiced concern about using sand, citing intestinal impaction, in over 40 years of lizard keeping, we've never had an incidence of this occur.

Window Cages

To allow hobbyists to make sunlight available to their herps, a "window cage" that slides in and out of an

opened window on extendable tracks has been developed. This should prove a real boon to apartment, condo, or city dwellers who would be otherwise unable to allow their lizards access to natural sunlight.

Rather than purchase a window cage, you may choose to build a less sophisticated, but suitably sized cage of wood and wire or of wire panels J-clamped together. This homemade cage can be hooked or wedged into a window. Although less convenient than a cage on tracks, it will more than suffice.

In all cases, when using a window cage, monitor the heat buildup, and provide a shaded area to which your lizards can retreat if they choose.

The Arid-Land Terrarium

Bearded dragons will thrive either in desert or savanna terraria. Properly arranged arid lands provide attractive habitats that stimulate both the interest of the hobbyist and the normal and social behaviors of the beardeds.

Cage Furniture
Rock ledges and caves, individual basking rocks, potted arid-land plants

Both heat lamps and full-spectrum lighting are suggested when dragons are kept indoors. (photo by Billy Griswold; from *Lizard Care A to Z*, page 25)

(including dried grasses), corkbark hiding areas, and cholla cactus skele-tons can be provided both for decoration and the psychological well being of your specimen(s). To promote low humidity, the terrarium should be in a well-ventilated area, and the top should be covered with screen.

How to Set Up a Naturalistic Arid-Land Terrarium

Choose a tank of suitable and adequate size. Be certain that the stand on which the terrarium will be placed can safely hold the weight.

Materials Needed

Terrarium and stand

Aquarium sealant to affix rock and limbs if necessary

Sand substrate

Small pots of drought-tolerant succulents like sanseveria or pachy-podium

2-in.-thick styrofoam insert, of preferred size (dried grasses will be inserted into this)

Phillips screwdriver or icepick to make holes (in which the grasses will stand) in styrofoam insert

Rocks and/or other terrarium furniture (rocks, contorted grape and manzanita branches, cholla skele-tons, corkbark [both flat and tubular sections], water receptacle) and camouflaged hide boxes

Undertank heater(s)

Terrarium top (metal-framed screen or wire top is best; full glass tops are not acceptable)

Lighting fixtures and bulbs (full spectrum fluorescent and heat-producing, directed-beam, color-corrected incandescent bulbs)

Small ventilation fan (optional)

Setup Procedure

1. Place the tank on its stand with the undertank heater in place at one end of the tank (follow directions carefully when placing and connecting the heaters).

2. If you want to add dried grasses as part of your decor, use the screwdriver to poke holes into the styrofoam, and insert the dried grasses into the holes. Put the styrofoam in place in the tank (you'll pour the sand around the insert later).

3. Position and seal in place any heavy cage furniture (rocks, limbs, etc.). This is a particularly important step, for if these items are just laid atop the surface sand, your dragons may burrow under them, and the rocks may settle on them. This can cause injury to or the death of the animals. Allow a minimum of 24 hours for sealant curing.

4. Pour the fine sand into the tank to the desired depth, carefully covering the styrofoam insert (taking care not to break the grasses—the dragons will do this soon enough!). Again, we suggest a depth of several inches. If you prefer a textured surface, you can mix a few pieces of variably sized river rock with the sand.

5. Position the plants. We prefer to leave the plants in their pots and sink the pots to the rim in the sand. This contains the moisture (and plant food) better when the plants are watered and prevents extensive areas of sand from becoming overly moist or saturated with fertilizer. If the plants begin suffering from insufficient light or other growth problems, replacing them is a simple matter. Alternatively, the plants can be removed from their pots and planted directly in the sand. Extreme care will then need to be used in watering and fertilizing, and replacing the plants is more difficult.

6. Arrange the water bowl and any remaining lightweight cage furniture either on the sand surface or partially buried, as desired. Depending on the number and compatibility of the specimens to be kept in the tank, from one to several secure hide boxes/hiding areas should be included.

7. Position and affix the lighting fixtures.

8. Plan to do some routine maintenance on the tank as a matter of course. For example, you will need to scoop the sand away from the styrofoam insert and replace the dried grasses as they are broken by the dragons. The plants will also need to be replaced occasionally.

Lighting and Heating
Bulbs that induce plant growth should be used for planted desert terraria. The directed beams of these can also provide sand-surface thermal gradients. Warmth can also be provided by using an undertank heater. Provide the desired thermal gradient by heating only one end of the terrarium. A heated end temperature of about 92–100° F will be fine. The cool end should be 80–85° F.

Outdoor Cages
Predators and Fire Ants
It should be mentioned at the outset that predators can be a problem for outdoor caging. Some animals, such as raccoons, opossums, domestic dogs, feral pigs, and other large species, may destroy screen barriers to get at either your lizards or your lizards' food. Feral rats and mice may chew through barriers. Even if actual preda-

tion on your beardeds does not occur, cage destruction can result in your pets escaping. Hawks, owls, crow family birds (corvids), roadrunners, shrikes, and even grackles may prey on specimens in open-topped cages. Covers preclude this possibility. Burrowing mammals such as shrews, voles, and moles may enter a cage from beneath and prey upon hibernating, or otherwise quiescent, beardeds or on clutches of eggs or newly emerging babies. A wire, wooden, or aluminum barrier buried 8- to 12-in. deep will usually protect your animals from these subterranean species. Take all necessary steps to preclude predation when—not after—building your outside cages.

Ants, and especially fire ants, are among the more serious lizard predators, and their exclusion is not only often initially overlooked but also downright difficult. These insects can quickly and efficiently ravage a collec-

tion, leaving behind dead and dying lizards. When situating your outdoor cage, avoid ant-prone areas of your yard, and immediately combat any indication of ant infiltration.

Outdoor Ring Cages

Ring cages are made from 3-ft.-high aluminum sheeting sunk one foot into the ground. They are circular and can be of any diameter, but we found that an 8- to 10-ft. diameter is ideal. Ring cages are relatively inexpensive.

The easiest way to outline and sink the sheeting is to use a post-hole digger attached to a 4.5-ft. length of twine. The other end of the twine is noosed loosely around a post tapped into the ground where the center of the cage is to be. By keeping the post-hole digger at the outer limit of the twine, it is a relatively simple matter to dig the foot-deep trench needed for the aluminum. No footer is needed for these cages. The aluminum sheeting is then set into the trench and leveled (this can be painstaking), and the two ends are riveted together. The trench

Dragons continually reposition themselves to best access the warming rays of the sun.

When alerted, dragons often curl their tail upward.

is filled on both sides, with particular care being given to the inside perimeter. After the trench is filled, the cage is essentially done. Hiding places/hibernacula of small diameter terra cotta drainage pipes can then be slanted into the ground, and several elevated perching areas of stones, logs, or other furniture added. Be certain that your dragons cannot leap from atop the cage furniture to the top of the ring and escape. Remember that after having basked in natural, unfiltered sunlight, a reptile is often more alert and agile than one kept indoors, even if you have provided ultraviolet light.

Plants for Indoor and Outdoor Cages

To have the very best naturalistic terraria, it is necessary to pay as much attention to the selection of your plants as of your animals. For indoor caging, remember that the nearer the tip of a leaf is to an incandescent light bulb, the more light and warmth are present. Thus, although the top of a sansevieria leaf may be receiving sufficient light for proper growth, the leaf

may be severely burned by the heat from the bulb. Choose and position plants and bulbs sympathetically. Be ready to change plant species from those requiring high light situations to species less demanding if growth becomes spindly or discolored.

Cacti

Many species and cultivars of common and easily grown cacti are available at stores and nurseries. Most grow well under intense artificial lighting, and some flower freely under such conditions. Despite their obvious armament, we have used cacti in our terraria over the decades and have never had any problems. Among others that grow well are the genus *Mammillaria*; several of the less lethally armed fishhook cacti, *Ferocactus*; star cacti, *Astrophytum*; and the comparatively spineless beaver-tail cacti, which are cultivars of the genus *Opuntia*.

Haworthias and Gasterias

These commonly grown nursery plants cluster readily into impressive, dwarfed thickets. Most of these lily relatives have leaves tipped with a rather weak spine and weakly serrate, spiny leaf edges. Of the two genera, the haworthias seem the easier to cultivate and require little in the way of winter cooling. Most of the haworthias thrive amid the rocks in an arid-land terrarium. Some have comparatively tender leaves, whereas the leaves of others are tough and almost indestructible. These plants have rosettes of leaves and may be either a squat, rather broadly opened rosette or rather tall with the leaves clasping the stem. The gasterias, on the other hand, enjoy cooler and drier conditions during the short days of winter. Most of the commonly offered species in both genera will grow well in somewhat less light than most cacti.

Sansevierias

The many species and cultivars of snakeplant or mother-in-law-tongue (genus *Sansevieria*) are ideal for brilliantly lighted savanna tanks. These African plants have been naturalized in many other areas of the world. Many are popular houseplants. There are species that have interesting cylindrical leaves, others that have curious spatulate leaves, and yet others that, while having normal leaves, form short ground-hugging rosettes. Those with which most of us are familiar have sturdy straplike leaves from 8 to 36 in. in height. The sansevierias are both hardy and drought tolerant. They can be propagated by offsets, by rooting leaf cuttings, and, more rarely, by seed. As would be expected, the plants need more water during their periods of active growth than when they are dormant. For those enthusiasts who like a little variety in terrarium plants, many of the sansevierias are available in both normal and variegated forms.

Pachypodiums

Smaller species of *Pachypodium*, spiny succulents from Africa and Madagascar, adapt well to the savanna terrarium. Sadly, *Pachypodium lamerei*, the species most often grown in pots, attains treelike proportions. The smallest species, *Pachypodium brevicaule*, is a cactiform species that is a remarkable rock-mimic with sparse leaves but beautiful yellow flowers. Between these are several ideal species of moderate size, differing structure, and superb hardiness, including *Pachypodium bispinosum* and *Pachy podium succulentum*.

The lesser bearded dragon is also referred to as the Rankin's bearded dragon and Lawson's bearded dragon.

Oddballs

Calibanus hookeri is a strange Mexican caudiciform (the ecological equivalent of cactus) plant that has numerous discrete tufts of raspy surfaced grassy leaves emerging from the caudex. It is hardy and ideal for the savanna terrarium.

Purslane or portulaca is sold by nurseries for both hanging garden baskets and as bedding plants. They are drought-tolerant succulents that are fragile and require very bright lighting. Because they are inexpensive and bear beautiful blossoms, these plants are occasionally used as expendable terrarium plants. Tortoises and herbivorous lizards readily eat both the foliage and blossoms.

The more brightly colored dragons are pretty animals indeed.

Feeding

Bearded dragons are omnivorous lizards. In nature, these lizards eat insects and gastropods (apparently from 40 to 75 percent of their diet is animal protein), berries and other available fruits, and some greenery. In captivity, dragons eat mealworms, giant mealworms, crickets, a variety of fruits, and finely chopped greens and vegetables of many kinds. Chopped greens (mustard, collard, beet), a little escarole, kale, and green cabbage are all good and nourishing food items. Chopped, fully thawed, frozen mixed vegetables and very little chopped fruit can also be given. (A food processor works wonders in the preparation of these foods.) The leaves and blossoms of dandelions and nasturtiums are also fine food items as would be a very occasional pinky (or just weaned) mouse.

Canned and prepared bearded dragon food is now available. Some of these preparations are touted as "complete diets," but we suggest that you augment them with fresh veggies and some insects. We suggest that you opt for dietary variety rather than dietary convenience when planning a bearded dragon's diet.

Dragon's Diet

Veggies (finely chopped)	Animal protein
Mustard greens	Gray crickets (*Acheta*)
Collard greens	Giant mealworms (*Zophobas*)
Beet greens	Mealworms (*Tenebrio*)
Kale	Waxworms (*Galleria*), sparingly
Bok choy	Pinkie mice (*Mus*), occasionally
Thawed mixed vegetables	Roaches (several genera) either
Fancy dark lettuces (not iceberg)	captive raised or from an
Sprouts (bean and alfalfa)	insecticide-free area
Green beans	
Peas (snow and other)	
Nasturtium leaves and flowers	
Hibiscus leaves and flowers	
Dandelion leaves and flowers	

Note: Because of the calcium-binding oxalic acid they contain, do not feed spinach or related plants to your dragons (see the Health section for more details on the importance of calcium levels).

Some dragons may opt to eat only a few favored items out of their daily offerings. This can be as unsatisfactory as simply offering a single item at each meal. Preferential selection becomes difficult when the veggies are finely chopped or mixed in a food processor. We should insist that our charges eat a healthy diet, all the while skewing dietary offerings toward what would be normal for them.

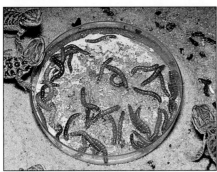

Chopped vegetables (top) and insects (bottom) are both important components of the diet for bearded dragons. (photo by Billy Griswold)

Although bearded dragons, and especially the babies, will pounce on and consume large food items like bigger beetles and chunks of fruit, big food items are not good for these lizards. Once in the stomach, too-large food items can cause the dragon to experience tetanic shock, tremors, and hind leg paralysis and can result in death.

Some breeders and keepers suggest that hatchling dragons not be fed veggies, but we feel that vegetables should be offered from the very first feeding. In this way, the dragons become used to greens and accept them readily throughout their life.

There is speculation that if fed in large amounts and over long periods, high-fat items—such as pinky and freshly weaned mice—may be harmful to the health of insectivorous or omnivorous lizards. It is always better to feed a varied natural or a quasi-natural diet to any captive reptile or amphibian, with bearded dragons being no exception. Mice, an unnatural, high-fat food as far as bearded dragons are concerned, should be offered only sparingly. Pinkies are useful as a food item to help postdeposition female dragons regain lost weight.

The Role of Natural, Unfiltered Sunlight in Calcium Utilization

Natural, unfiltered sunlight unquestionably provides the best possible lighting (and heat) for bearded dragons. It provides other benefits as well. Ultraviolet rays are known to

26

promote natural behavior (UV-A) and to promote the synthesis of a vitamin D3 precursor in the skin (UV-B). The complex interactions between D3 and proper calcium utilization by your dragon (and other omnivorous/herbivorous lizards) continue to be studied but are known to be intertwined.

When temperatures are sufficiently warm, we suggest that you allow your dragon to partake of natural unfiltered sunlight when possible. Even though daily availability would certainly be best for the lizard, occasional availability is far better than none.

We suggest the use of UV-A/UV-B emitting bulbs when natural sunlight is not available or is only sporadically available. Make certain that the bulbs are 12–15 in. above the basking area and replace them every 9 months.

Inland bearded dragons have whitish or pinkish mouth linings.

Vitamin–Mineral Supplements

There is little doubt that vitamin–mineral supplements—most notably vitamin D3 and calcium—are necessary for bone development, eggshell formation, and the general well being of your lizards. The amount and the method of administration are less precisely agreed upon. If the supplement you choose contains phosphorus, check to make certain that the calcium:phosphorous ratio is 2:1.

Bearded dragons with daily (or even weekly) access to natural sunlight will need fewer supplements than those kept indoors. Rapidly growing baby bearded dragons and ovulating females require supplements with more frequency than dragons at other stages of their lives.

We have found the following guidelines to work well:

We provide daily supplementation of D3 and calcium (actually we use a multivitamin—Osteoform) from hatching until the dragons are about one-quarter grown.

We provide supplements every second day from when the dragons are one-quarter grown until they are about one-half grown.

We provide supplements about every fourth day when they are from one-half grown to when they are adult.

We provide vitamin–mineral supplements to adult dragons weekly, but ovulating females who need extra calcium for eggshell formation are given supplements twice weekly.

27

The supplement may be blended into the prepared veggies and/or applied to crickets in the "shake and bake" method (the crickets are placed into a jar or bag with a little additive and shaken about until a fine patina of the supplement coats each insect). Feed the insects to the lizards as soon after dusting as possible.

"Gut-Loading" Food Insects

Unless they are continuously fed a diet of nutritious foods, insects will provide your lizards with little more than chitinous bulk. Feed all insects well. Several cricket diets that are high in calcium and vitamin D3 are now commercially available. This diet is also suitable for mealworms of both species. Food insects will also eat many vegetables and cereals as well as lab-rodent chow. Food insects will also require a source of water or moisture from fruit such as apples, carrots, and oranges. To ensure that your bearded dragons get the greatest benefit from the insects you provide them, feed the insects to the lizards as quickly as possible after removing them from their food source.

Water

Bearded dragons seem to metabolize much of their moisture requirements from the fresh plant material that they eat. However, they will also drink from a dish. In low-humidity areas, a shallow dish of fresh water may be kept with the bearded dragons at all times. In areas where high humidity prevails, to keep cage humidity as low as possible, it is better to offer your dragons water for a few hours every second day, after the dragons have warmed up and begun their daily behavioral regimen.

The male (foreground) of this pair of inland dragons is displaying to the female.

Conditioning and Breeding Bearded Dragons

Although bearded dragons often breed well in captivity with little concerted preparation, some guidelines should be followed to ascertain their reproductive cycling.

Males, aggressive toward other males at all times, become savagely aggressive toward other male *Pogona* during the breeding season. To avoid problems, keep only a single male to one to three females in an indoor cage. Even in large outside cages, unless there are ample hiding spots and visual barriers, keeping more than a single male to a cage may affect not only your success at breeding but also the health of the males.

Sexing Your Dragon

It is difficult to impossible to reliably sex baby and juvenile bearded dragons. Sexual differences in adult dragons are present but are comparative and can be minimal.

Adult male dragons often have:	Adult female dragons have:
A wider tail base (to accommodate the hemipenes) and wider cloacal opening	Narrower tail base and narrow cloacal opening
A broader, more strongly triangular head	Less strongly triangular head (narrower posteriorly)
Enlarged (but very irregularly placed and often darkened) femoral and preanal pores	Smaller and usually not darkened femoral pores
Darkened beards, especially during breeding season	Lighter colored beards
Less robust build	Heavy build (inordinately so when gravid)
Enhanced aggressive behavior (especially during breeding season)	Less aggressive; use circumduction (arm-waving) extensively

Cycling

Under natural conditions, the life cycles of lizards are influenced by the seasonal climatic changes. Influencing factors include photoperiod, temperature, rainfall, and relative humidity. Even in captivity, certain of these cyclic stimuli can and should be approximated when preparing your dragons for breeding. All except rainfall seem significant to the desert- and dry-savanna-dwelling bearded dragons.

The term *photoperiod* simply refers to the hours of daylight (as opposed to the hours of darkness) in any given day. Photoperiod is more seasonally variable at (or near) the poles than at the equator. The hours of daylight increase as winter gives way to spring and spring to summer and then decrease again in the autumn. Check the weather page in your local newspaper for the exact sunrise and sunset times, and periodically (about weekly) alter the numbers of hours that your cage is artificially illuminated. If you happen to be keeping your lizard in outside caging, allow Mother Nature to dictate photoperiod naturally. Of course, because they are a heliothermic species, brilliant illumination is necessary to induce peak activity in your dragons.

Although usually placid, some inland bearded dragons will attempt to bite. The distended beard and open mouth reflect this defensive male's attitude.

The triangular head of the inland dragon is very evident.

This is a young male inland bearded dragon of Bob Mailloux's sandfire morph.

The female red flame dragon (far left), when bred with the male sandfire, produced a large clutch similar in color to the two 8 month olds on the right.

Temperatures, both daily and seasonal, can be altered with the prudent use of lights and/or heating elements. Bearded dragons are desert and dry-savanna lizards that are well adapted to hot summer temperatures and somewhat cooler winter ones. A drop of nighttime temperature is also permissible.

Not all dragon eggs are created equal. To produce healthy eggs that develop into robust hatchlings, your breeding bearded dragons must be in overall good health (it is better not to breed dragons in suboptimal health). Dragons seem to breed more reliably and to produce healthier eggs and hatchlings when they have undergone a 2-month-long period of winter cooling (not hibernation—just cooling!).

Generally speaking, in midwinter, you should provide the lowest humidity, the fewest hours of daylight, and the lowest nighttime temperatures. Ten hours of daylight should be the minimum. Allow the temperatures to cool to 80° F under the basking light, and to 60–65° F at night. Reduce the feeding, both in quantity at a given meal and in frequency. When temperatures again warm, increase meal size and frequency. Your lizards should be fed most heavily from early spring during the longest and warmest days of the year. Heavy springtime feedings are especially important for female dragons that need additional weight to enable them to breed.

Be sure to provide plenty of calcium and D3 throughout the year. These additives are especially important at the time of eggshell formation by adult female dragons and for proper bone development and the growth of hatchlings and juveniles.

To restrain receptive females, male inland dragons bite their nape. (photo by Billy Griswold)

Breeding

Courtship involves much body language by the male dragon, including beard distension, head-bobbing, body inflation, and circumduction. Male dragons usually restrict the escape of a receptive female by biting the back of the female's neck. During the height of the breeding season, this can cause open wounds that may need medical attention.

The Eggs

All bearded dragons are oviparous. That is, they reproduce by laying eggs. Their eggs have a pliable (and permeable) parchmentlike shell. Depending on the species, a clutch may consist of from 6 to about 25 eggs; the smaller dragon species usually produce fewer eggs than the larger species. Depending on the number of eggs she is carrying, a heavily gravid female

Fertile eggs are white and turgid. (photo by Billy Griswold; from *Lizard Care A to Z*, page 58, top right)

This gravid female inland dragon is digging her nesting chamber in moist sand.

bearded dragon may look only reasonably heavy or may appear positively fat.

An adult female will usually produce four to six clutches a year (at 3- to 4-week intervals) for the first several years of her life. Unless she is in top-notch condition when she enters the egging cycle, she can be quickly debilitated. Feed an egging female heavily on a nutritious diet between depositions.

The Deposition Site

In nature, female lizards rather carefully choose the site that they instinctively feel will best suit the eggs for the approximately 60 days of incubation. Oviposition occurs during the hours of daylight, often in mid to late afternoon. Suitable sites must be provided for gravid captive dragons. Bearded dragons of all species dig rather extensive nesting burrows. They dig the burrow with the forefeet, removing the loosened soil with the rear feet. When the female feels the hole is deep enough, she will reverse her position and lay her eggs with only her nose showing. Following deposition, the burrow is methodically refilled. The main criterion for the completion of a nesting burrow seems to be that the soil is soft enough to be worked with relative ease and is of a consistency that the burrow retains its shape while being dug. If an obstruction is encountered while digging, the female will often leave the site, choose another, and begin over. A nesting burrow is often from 5 in. (smaller dragon species) to more than 12 in. (larger dragon species) long. The burrows may be dug laterally into the side of a provided pile of sandy loam or diagonally downward into the soil.

A female inland dragon has begun laying her clutch. (photo by Billy Griswold; from *Lizard Care A to Z*, page 58, top left)

If a suitable nesting site is not provided, dragons (and most other oviparous reptiles) may retain the eggs until natural deposition is difficult or impossible. At that point in time a hormonal stimulant may need to be administered or egg-removal surgery performed.

The eggs of smaller dragon species may take only 42 days to incubate, whereas those of the larger forms may occasionally take 80 or more days.

In some cases, especially where suitable deposition sites are difficult to find, females may nest communally. The eggs of a given clutch often all hatch on the same day, but occasionally several days are involved.

Egg Incubation— An Overview

Following deposition, remove the eggs as soon as possible for incubation. It seems best, but may not be as critical as we once thought, if the orientation in which the egg was found is not changed. (In other words, just to be

Inland dragon eggs are about twice as long as they are wide. (photo by Billy Griswold; from *Lizard Care A to Z*, page 58, bottom left)

safe, keep the same side up.) Infertile eggs may be present in any given clutch. Additionally, a certain percentage of embryonic mortality should be expected.

Perlite and vermiculite have proven to be ideal incubation media. Moisten whichever you choose to use with four parts of water to five or six parts of the dry perlite or vermiculite (by volume). It should be moist enough to clump when squeezed but should not drip water. Place 1–1.5 in. of the moistened medium in the bottom of a plastic shoe box. The eggs of bearded dragons seem to incubate most successfully if they are one-half to two-thirds buried in the substrate. Simply make a depression for each egg with a fingertip. Once the eggs are in place, put the lid on the shoe box and cup it in the incubator. A shallow open dish of water in the incubator will help keep the relative humidity high.

If the medium is too dry or too wet, the permeable eggshells of bearded dragons readily allow desicca-tion or overhydration of the eggs. Either can cause the death of the embryo. Watch the eggs closely during incubation. If the eggs begin to collapse, increase the moisture slightly; if they get turgid and slick, decrease the moisture. Do note, however, that even under ideal incubation conditions, when full-term is neared, dimpling and a concurrent lack of eggshell turgidity is normal. Some eggs may go full-term but, if the embryo is weak, fail to hatch. Some of these babies may be saved by carefully slitting the eggshell. If the baby within is viable, it may emerge within a day or two, but, even with extra care, weak hatchlings often succumb within a few days following emergence.

The sex of many lizard species is determined by the temperature at which the egg is incubated. This is called temperature-dependent sex determination. This does not seem to be true with bearded dragons. Both males and females are produced at all suitable incubation temperatures. Bearded dragons will hatch successfully at incubator temperatures between 81 and 85° F; 83–84° F is optimal.

Making Your Own Incubator

The following materials are needed for one incubator:

1 wafer thermostat (obtainable from feed stores; these are commonly used in incubators for chicks)

1 thermometer

1 Styrofoam cooler—one with thick sides (a fish-shipping box is ideal)

1 heat tape

A small commercially made incubator. (photo by Billy Griswold; from *Lizard Care A to Z*, page 60, bottom)

1 electrical cord and wall plug

3 wire nuts

1 piece of 1 × 2 in. mesh hardware cloth, large enough for a u-shaped shelf

Poke a hole through the lid of the Styrofoam cooler and suspend the thermostat from the inside. The temperature adjustment handle of the thermostat should protrude through the lid and be easily worked without opening the incubator. The two wires should be inside. Add another hole through the lid for a thermometer so that you can check on the inside temperature without opening the top. If there's no flange on the thermometer to keep it from slipping through the hole in the lid, wind a rubber band around the thermometer several times to form a flange.

Your goal is to wire the thermostat between the heat tape and the electrical cord in order to regulate the amount of heat produced by the heat tape.

Cut the electrical cord off the heat tape, leaving about 18 in. of the cord on the heat tape. Make a hole through the side of the Styrofoam box, about 5 in. below the top edge. Pull the electrical cord through the hole, leaving the plug end outside (don't plug it in just yet!). Strip off about a half-inch of the insulation from the wiring at the cut end, and separate the two wires for a few inches.

Coil the heat tape loosely in the bottom of the Styrofoam box, making sure that it doesn't cross over itself at any point. Coil the tape so the recently cut end is near the electrical cord. Strip off about a half-inch of the insulation from the end of the wiring, and separate the two wires for a few inches.

Using one of the wire nuts, connect one of the red wires of the thermostat to one of the electrical wires of the heat tape. Use a second nut to connect the second red wire of the thermostat to one of the wires of the electrical cord. The third nut is used to connect the second wire of the

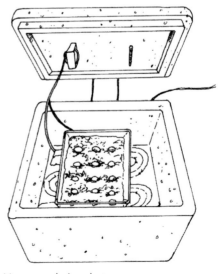

Homemade incubator.

electrical cord to the second wire of the heat tape (in effect, reestablishing part of the original wiring between the heat tape and its electrical cord).

That's all there is to it. Put the lid on the cooler and plug in the thermostat/heater. Wait half an hour and check the temperature. The L-shaped pin on the top of the thermostat is the rheostat; turn it to increase or decrease the temperature inside your new incubator. You want the inside to be 80–86°F.

Once you have the temperature regulated, add your hardware cloth "shelf" and put the container of eggs atop the shelf. Close the egg container.

Check the temperature daily and add a little water to the incubating medium if it gets dry (it should stay damp enough to stick together when you stick your finger into it, or when you push it into a little heap with your finger). Take care to add the water to the medium, not onto the eggs. The preferred humidity is 100 percent. Placing an open deli container, half filled with water, onto the hardware cloth shelf will also help maintain the humidity.

How do you know if the eggs are fertile? By the end of the first week, those eggs that are not fertile will turn yellow, harden, and begin to collapse.

Remove and discard them. Those that are fertile will remain white and turgid to the touch.

At the end of the incubation period—which may be as little as 42 days for some species but is usually 60, 70, or even 80 days for inland bearded dragons—the babies will cut a slit in their egg with an egg tooth on the tip of their snout.

After pipping, the babies will remain in the eggs for from several hours to more than a day. After hatching, they should be removed to another terrarium and, once active, offered food, a sunning spot, and water. They should shed within a few days.

Care of the Young

In the wild, baby bearded dragons emerging from a nest would quickly scatter far and wide. They are seldom able to do so in captivity.

Typically, baby dragons are grouped, a dozen or more to a plastic blanket box set up with a paper towel substrate, basking areas, and hiding areas. Anthropomorphically, there is hardly anything cuter than a group of hatchling bearded dragons, scrambling over each other to partake of the

It may be several hours after pipping before baby dragons emerge fully from their eggs. (photo by Billy Griswold)

This group of baby inland dragons is only a few days old. (photo by Billy Griswold; from *Lizard Care A to Z*, page 58, bottom right)

hot spots, to reach fresh food, or to ascend to the highest point in their cage. But cute, in this case, equates to stress. Numbers of baby dragons in a cage can cause overt aggression and has been associated with stress-related proliferation of endoparasites, which, in turn, cause digestive problems. We suggest that dragons be sized in the largest cages possible, that they be carefully watched for aggressive behavior (and segregated when necessary), and that the cause of any loose and sticky stools (usually parasites) be immediately addressed.

Despite these problems and the fact that hatchling and juvenile bearded dragons can be aggressive enough to cause injury to each other, if it is necessary and if you watch them closely, they can be successfully reared in groups. To prevent overt aggression, it is important to keep all baby dragons in any given group approximately the same size, to remove the most aggressive ones, and to keep the babies very well fed. A well-fed baby dragon will be less inclined to nip and injure the toes and tailtips of its cage mates—even those of similar size. Severed tailtips or toes will not regenerate.

By placing the fastest growing, largest, and most aggressive babies into their own size groups and by feeding heavily, the potential for many problems will be considerably lessened.

A Note on Feeding Baby Bearded Dragons

Hatchling bearded dragons of all species have surprisingly robust appetites. We feel that it is important that they are fed a minimum of once daily, and that twice daily is better. When hungry, baby bearded dragons will attempt to eat prey items that are far too large for their well being. A meal of several small crickets, mealworms, and mixed veggies is far better (and safer) for baby dragons than a meal consisting of a single large insect. They will swallow large insects, but this isn't a good idea.

Several hours following the eating of a proportionately large prey item, baby dragons have occasionally undergone convulsions and partial paralysis that has usually resulted in the death of the dragon.

Be safe. Provide more frequent feedings of smaller prey.

Endoparasites

The presence of internal parasites in lizards from the wild is a foregone conclusion. However, few hobbyists realize that captive-bred and hatched lizards may also harbor endoparasites and other pathogens. *Pseudomonas*, roundworms, pinworms, nematodes, tapeworms, and/or parasitic protozoans are typical endoparasites.

Endoparasites can be diagnosed by fecal exams. Whether or not your veterinarian treats your lizard for endoparasites may depend on the behavior and condition of the lizard. Certainly the problems created by

endoparasitic loads in weakened lizards need to be addressed promptly. However, if the specimen in question is bright-eyed, alert, and feeding well and has a good color, you and your vet may agree to forego treating the animal. Endoparasitic loads can actually diminish if you keep the cage of your specimen scrupulously clean, thereby preventing reinfestation.

Getting rid of endoparasites means administering a substance that is toxic to the parasites in dosages that will not harm your lizard. Obviously, dosages must be accurate, which is why you need to take your animal to your veterinarian. To begin with, your

This is a large female red flame dragon owned by Liz Craig and Matthew Steen.

veterinarian can accurately weigh your lizard, whose weight determines the dosage of medication to be used. It is also very easy for a layperson to miscalculate metric conversions or to fail to actually get the correct dosage into the lizard. The result may be fatal or futile. Let your reptile veterinarian do the work for which he or she was trained. So that you may discuss possible endoparasitic treatments with your veterinarian, some sample treatments and dosages appear at the end of this chapter.

Coccidia

The presence of coccidia in dragons' guts is an insidious and persistent problem. An overabundance of these telosporidian protozoans can impair digestion and cause your dragon to be listless and run down and finally can, though direct and secondary infections, cause death. Bearded dragons have their very own species of coccidium, *Isospora amphiboluri*. Because these parasites do not require an outside host to complete their life cycle, immense numbers can quickly build up. If your dragon is dull-eyed and listless and has loose or smelly stools that stick to the anal opening, coccidia (or other endoparasites) should be suspected, and a veterinary assessment performed.

Ectoparasites

External parasites are less problematic to treat than endoparasites. Both mites and ticks are occasionally seen, but both are easily expunged. Ticks, which are deflated and seedlike when empty but rounded and bladderlike when engorged, may be removed manually.

They embed their mouthparts deeply when feeding, and if merely pulled from the lizard, these may break off in the wound. It is best to dust them individually with Sevin powder first and then to return a few minutes later and pull the ticks off gently with a pair of tweezers. Mites may be combatted with Sevin dust (best in arid climates) or with Ivomectin mist. An inch-square piece of No-Pest strip, placed atop the screen cover of the cage, will work as well. (Be certain to remove the water bowl for the three days you use the No-Pest strip.) In most cases, total eradication of mites will take two or more treatments at 9-day intervals. These treatments have the potential of being debilitating or fatal to hatchling dragons. Seek the services of a reptile-oriented vet, especially when treating young *Pogona*.

Metabolic Bone Disease

The technical names for metabolic bone disease (MBD) are nutritional secondary hyperthyroidism and fibrous osteodystrophy. In simplified terms, MBD is the result of too little calcium in the diet and not enough vitamin D3, the vitamin that enables the body to utilize calcium. In dragons, MBD's basic symptoms are tetanic convulsions or spastic twitching of the extended limbs, foreshortened and softened jawbones, and swollen, pliable limbs. Left untreated, your animal will die.

To exist, a dragon needs a certain level of calcium in the blood. When the level of blood calcium drops below a certain percentage, the parathyroid glands then begin drawing calcium out of the bones and moving that calcium to the bloodstream to maintain the levels there. As the bones lose their rigidity, parts of them become overlaid with a fibrous tissue to compensate for the loss of strength—hence the swollen, "chubby" look to the face and the limbs.

The bones are very easily broken at this point. In its early stages, MBD is treatable. Vitamin–mineral supplements are crucial; veterinary assessment is mandatory.

Respiratory Ailments

Although well-acclimated, properly maintained bearded dragons are not prone to respiratory ailments, if they are stressed, or only marginally healthy and are subjected to unnatural periods of cold (especially damp cold), they may occasionally break down with colds or pneumonia. Some respiratory ailments may also be associated with the weakening brought about by a heavy endoparasite burden.

Respiratory ailments are indicated by sneezing, lethargic demeanor, and unnaturally rapid, often shallow, breathing. As the disease progresses, rasping and bubbling may accompany each of your lizard's breaths. At this stage, the respiratory ailment is often critical and can be fatal.

Begin by separating the ill lizard from any cage mates, placing it in its own cage, and then elevating the illuminated basking area (NOT the entire cage) to about 110° F. The more optimal its surroundings, the better able the specimen is to deal with a respiratory ailment.

The rest of the cage should be maintained at 85–90° F. If the symptoms of respiratory distress do not greatly lessen within a day or two, do not delay any longer. Call your veterinarian, and take your lizard to him or her for antibiotic treatment.

There are many "safe" drugs available, but some respiratory ailments do not respond well to these. The newer aminoglycoside drugs, and others, newer still, are more effective, but they are correspondingly more dangerous. There is little latitude in dosage amounts, and the lizard must be well hydrated to ensure against renal (kidney) damage. The injection site for aminoglycosides should be anterior to midbody to avoid damaging the kidneys.

Other Maladies

Several other diseases and maladies may occur rarely. Among these are:

- Mineralization of internal organs: This is caused by the overmetabolization of calcium and is known as hypercalcemia. A treatment has now been developed but is both lengthy and expensive. Treatment requires about 2 weeks of monitoring by a veterinarian. There is a fine line between too much and not enough calcium and vitamin D3. Once diagnosed and corrected, you'll need to reduce both calcium and D3 intake by your specimen. If untreated or too far advanced, taking supplements can be a fatal problem.
- Hypoglycemia: This relates to low blood sugar. Stress or pancreatic dysfunction can be the causative agent. The stress factor is cor-

rectable; the pancreatic dysfunction, most commonly caused by an insulin-secreting tumor, usually is not.

- Hindquarter paralysis: See MBD symptoms, page 39, and too-large food items, page 26.

Medical Treatments for Internal Parasites

Because of the complexities of identification of endoparasites and the need to weigh specimens for them to be treated accurately, the eradication of internal parasites is best left to a qualified reptile veterinarian. These are a few of the recommended medications and dosages.

Amoebas and Trichomonads

For amoebas and trichomonads, a singular treatment of 40–50 mg/kg of metronidazole is given orally. The treatment is repeated in 2 weeks. Dimetridazole can also be used, but the dosage is very different. For 5 days, 40–50 mg/kg of dimetrizadole is administered daily. The treatment is then repeated in 2 weeks. All treatments with both medications are administered once daily.

Coccidia

Many treatments are available. The dosages of sulfadiazine, sulfamerazine, and sulfamethazine are identical. Administer 75 mg/kg the first day, then follow up for the next 5 days with 45 mg/kg. All treatments are administered orally and once daily. Sulfadimethoxine is also effective. The initial dosage is 90 mg/kg orally to be followed on the next 5 days with 45 mg/kg orally. All dosages are administered once daily. Trimethoprim-sulfa may also be used by administering 30 mg/kg once daily for 7 days.

Cestodes (Tapeworms)

Several effective treatments are available. Bunamidine may be administered orally at a dosage of 50 mg/kg. A second treatment occurs in 14 days. Niclosamide, given orally at a dosage of 150 mg/kg, is also effective. A second treatment is given in 2 weeks. Finally, praziquantel may be administered either orally or intramuscularly. The dosage is 5–8 mg/kg and is to be repeated in 14 days.

Trematodes (Flukes)

Praziquantel at 8 mg/kg may be administered either orally or intramuscularly. The treatment is repeated in 2 weeks.

Nematodes (Roundworms)

Several effective treatments are available. Levamisole, an injectable intraperitoneal treatment, should be administered at a dosage of 10 mg/kg, and the treatment should be repeated in 2 weeks. Ivermectin, injected intramuscularly in a dosage of 200 mg/kg, is effective. The treatment is to be repeated in 2 weeks. Ivermectin can be toxic to certain taxa. Thiabendazole and fenbendazole have similar dosages. Both are administered orally at 50–100 mg/kg and repeated in 14 days. Mebendazole is administered orally at a dosage of 20–25 mg/kg and is repeated in 14 days.

Special Interest Groups

Herpetological Societies

Reptile and amphibian enthusiasts can meet like-minded people and learn more about their hobby through herp societies, monthly magazines, and professional associations, in addition to commercial functions such as herp expos.

Herpetological societies (or clubs) exist in major cities in North America, Europe, and other areas of the world. Most have monthly meetings, some publish newsletters, and many host or sponsor field trips or picnics, or indulge in various other interactive functions. Among the members are enthusiasts of varying expertise. Information about these clubs can often be found by querying pet shop employees, high school science teachers, university biology department professors, or curators or employees at the department of herpetology at local museums and zoos. All such clubs welcome inquiries and new members.

Two of the professional herpetological societies are:

Society for the Study of Amphibians and Reptiles (SSAR)
Department of Zoology
Miami University
Oxford, OH 45056

Herpetologist's League
c/o Texas National Heritage Program
Texas Parks and Wildlife Department
4200 Smith School Road
Austin, TX 78744

The SSAR publishes two quarterly journals: *Herpetological Review*, which contains husbandry, range extensions, news on ongoing field studies, and the like, and *Journal of Herpetology*, which contains articles more oriented toward academic herpetology.

Hobbyist magazines that publish articles on all aspects of herpetology and herpetoculture (including lizards) are:

Reptiles
P O Box 6050
Mission Viejo, CA 92690

Reptile and Amphibian Hobbyist
Third and Union Avenues
Neptune City, NJ 07753

These hobbyist magazines also carry classified ads and news about herp expos.

On-line services on the Internet have proliferated in the last few years. Simply type "reptiles and amphibians" or "bearded dragons" and click on your search engine.

Glossary

Ambient temperature: The temperature of the surrounding environment.

Anterior: Toward the front.

Anus: The external opening of the cloaca; the vent.

Caudal: Pertaining to the tail.

Circumduction: The stylized waving of a forelimb as a gesture of appeasement.

Cloaca: The common chamber into which digestive, urinary, and reproductive systems empty and which itself opens exteriorly through the vent or anus.

Deposition: As used here, the laying of the eggs.

Deposition site: The spot chosen by the female to lay her eggs.

Diurnal: Active by day.

Dorsal: Pertaining to the back; upper surface.

Dorsolateral: Pertaining to the upper sides.

Dorsum: The upper surface.

Femoral pores: Enlarged, pheromone-emitting scales on the underside of the femur.

Genus: A taxonomic classification of a group of species having similar characteristics. The genus falls between the next higher designation of family and the next lower designation of species.

Genera is the plural of genus. The generic name is always capitalized when written.

Gravid: The reptilian equivalent of mammalian pregnancy.

Heliothermic: A species that basks in the sunlight to attain thermal optimums.

Hemipenes: The dual copulatory organs of male lizards and snakes.

Hemipenis: The singular form of hemipenes.

Juvenile: A young or immature specimen.

Lateral: Pertaining to the side.

Middorsal: Pertaining to the middle of the back.

Midventral: Pertaining to the center of the belly or abdomen.

Oviparous: Reproducing by means of eggs that hatch after laying.

Poikilothermic: A species with no internal body temperature regulation. The old term was *cold-blooded*.

Posterior: Toward the rear.

Preanal pores: A series of pores, often in the shape of an anteriorly directed chevron, located anterior to the anus.

Saxicolous: Rock-dwelling.

Serrate: Sawlike.

Species: A group of similar creatures that produce viable young when breeding. The taxonomic designation that falls beneath genus and above subspecies.

Subcaudal: Beneath the tail.

Subdigital: Beneath the toes.

Subspecies: The subdivision of a species. A race that may differ slightly in color, size, scalation, or other criteria.

Terrestrial: Land-dwelling.

Thermoregulate: To regulate (body) temperature by choosing a warmer or cooler environment.

Tympanum: The external eardrum.

Vent: The external opening of the cloaca; the anus.

Venter: The underside of a creature; the belly.

Ventral: Pertaining to the undersurface or belly.

Ventrolateral: Pertaining to the sides of the venter (belly).

Note: Other scientific definitions are contained in the following two volumes:

Peters, James A. 1964. *Dictionary of Herpetology*. New York: Hafner Publishing Co.

Wareham, David C. 1993. *The Reptile and Amphibian Keeper's Dictionary*. London: Blandford.

Index